How Christmas Saved the World from Aliens

Madison, Grant, Emma & Grant,

HERE WE GO STEELERS!!

Jay W. Foreman

Written by Jay W. Foreman, Illustrated by Mark Sasser

CrossBooks™
A Division of LifeWay
1663 Liberty Drive
Bloomington, IN 47403
www.crossbooks.com
Phone: 1-866-879-0502

First published by CrossBooks 10/15/2010

ISBN: 978-1-6150-7585-0

Library of Congress Control Number: 2010939412

Printed in the United States of America

This book is printed on acid-free paper.

CROSSBOOKS

DEDICATED TO MY
NIECES & NEPHEWS:
ELIZABETH, BRIANNA & ABBY
BLACKBURN, LUKE & LOGAN LEWIS
AND TO MY GOOD FRIEND:
GRACE SASSER

Grab some cookies and
a mug of hot cocoa
because you're about to
hear a story that not
too many people know.

It's about Alyak and Relyt,
two aliens from space,
and how their view
of Christmas saved
the human race.

THESE ALIENS ARE FROM THE
PLANET STLOC IN A GALAXY
KNOWN AS SASTYKE,
AND THEY HAVE A NASTY
REPUTATION FOR INVADING
PLANETS THEY DON'T LIKE.

The planet Earth was on their list: to conquer or to spare? They decided to do some research in order to be fair.

Alyak sent Relyt to Earth to study the humans' ways. They felt this would be done best by examining holidays.

It was agreed that Relyt would come to Earth and observe humans for one year. He hid in the background of the humans' world to avoid causing fear.

AFTER A YEAR, RELYT RETURNED
TO STLOC TO REPORT ON HUMAN
HOLIDAY TRADITIONS.
THE FOLLOWING IS RELYT'S REPORT
TO ALYAK ON WHICH THEY
WOULD BASE THEIR DECISIONS:

"THE FIRST CELEBRATED HOLIDAY
I SAW CAUGHT ME OFF GUARD.
I SAW MEN BUYING FLOWERS
FOR WOMEN, BOXES OF
CHOCOLATES AND CARDS.

IT IS CALLED VALENTINE'S DAY,
BUT I WAS NOT IMPRESSED
WITH HOW IT WENT.
WOMEN COMPLAINED THAT
THEIR GIFTS WERE TOO SMALL,
AND MEN GRIPED ABOUT HOW
MUCH MONEY THEY SPENT.

I EVEN SAW ONE MAN WEAR
A GIANT DIAPER—HE WAS
TRYING TO IMITATE CUPID.
IF YOU ASK ME, IT DIDN'T
WORK, AND HE JUST ENDED
UP LOOKING STUPID.

VALENTINE'S DAY IS SUPPOSED TO BE ABOUT COUPLES CELEBRATING THE LOVE THAT THEY NEED, BUT EVERYTHING I SAW DEMONSTRATED NOTHING MORE THAN GREED.

"THE NEXT HOLIDAY CAME IN
THE SPRING, AND I HAD TO
WAKE AT THE CRACK OF DAWN
TO SEE CHILDREN SEARCHING
FOR PAINTED EGGS AND TOYS
HIDDEN ON THEIR LAWNS.

THESE EGGS WERE HIDDEN
BY A GIANT RABBIT CALLED
THE EASTER BUNNY.
A GIANT RABBIT HIDING PAINTED EGGS?
TO ME, THAT'S JUST FUNNY!

I BELIEVE THIS HOLIDAY IS CALLED
EASTER, AND IT'S SUPPOSED
TO BE A DAY OF JOY,
BUT I WITNESSED BOYS AND
GIRLS FIGHTING TO FIND THE
BEST EGGS AND TOYS!

"Just when I thought things couldn't get worse, along came the Fourth of July. Would you believe that humans celebrate by launching tiny rockets into the sky?

I HOPE IT'S IMPORTANT TO
THEM TO SEE SHINY LIGHTS
AND HEAR, 'BOOM!'
BECAUSE MOST OF THE HUMANS
I SAW SET OFF FIREWORKS ENDED
UP IN AN EMERGENCY ROOM.

"HALLOWEEN WAS THE NEXT HOLIDAY. KIDS DRESSED UP AND KNOCKED ON DOORS FOR CANDY. I BLENDED RIGHT IN AMONG ALL OF THE COSTUMES. THIS REALLY CAME IN HANDY!

AFTER THE KIDS HAD FILLED
THEIR BAGS WITH AS MUCH
CANDY AS THEY COULD TAKE
THEY WENT HOME AND ATE
ALL THEY COULD UNTIL EACH
ONE HAD A STOMACH ACHE!

"Next I saw them eat turkey on Thanksgiving. This holiday seemed to be the most absurd. I'll spare you the details like where they stick the stuffing when they're preparing the bird!

EVERYONE EATS AS MUCH AS THEY CAN AND EATS MORE UNTIL THEY FEEL SICK. THEN THEY TRY TO WATCH FOOTBALL ON TV, BUT FALL ASLEEP BEFORE THE OPENING KICK."

Alyak held up a hand
and stopped Relyt at this
point in his review.
He said, "You've done a great job
describing the humans. I don't
feel there's a need to continue.

You've shown that humans
are greedy, selfish, careless,
undisciplined, and lazy.
Why shouldn't we invade
Earth? Human life seems
meaningless and crazy."

"I thought so too," replied Relyt, "until I experienced Christmas in December. That's when I witnessed something that I will always remember.

"I KNOW THAT HUMANS
HAVE THEIR FAULTS BUT ALL
OTHER RACES DO TOO.
I HAVE NEVER SEEN A CHRISTMAS
BEFORE WHEN PEOPLE
CHANGE LIKE THEY DO.

THESE SAME PEOPLE WHO
WERE GREEDY AND SELFISH
EARLIER IN THE YEAR
BECOME DIFFERENT PEOPLE
AROUND THIS TIME—I BELIEVE
THEY CALL IT *CHRISTMAS CHEER.*

EACH HUMAN SMILES, LAUGHS,
AND GIVES GIFTS TO EVERYONE.
I SAW HUMANS, YOUNG
AND OLD, DOING GOOD
DEEDS AND HAVING FUN.

"THEY SANG, DANCED, AND PARTIED. ON THEIR HOUSES THEY STRUNG LIGHTS. THEN THEY ALL WALKED AROUND TO TAKE IN THE BEAUTIFUL SIGHTS.

FOR A BRIEF TIME, THE GOOD
NATURE OF HUMANS IS SHOWN.
IF HUMANS CAN BE THIS
GOOD, I RECOMMEND WE
LEAVE THIS PLANET ALONE."

"I don't understand," replied Alyak. "If humans are so wonderful at Christmas, why don't they stay this way?" "The truth is," answered Relyt, "humans have a short memory, and in January they start to stray.

THEY FALL BACK INTO THEIR OLD
HABITS OF PETTINESS AND BLAME.
THEY FORGET WHO THEY
WERE AT CHRISTMAS, WHICH
REALLY IS A SHAME.

"But that's the beauty of Christmas—it comes back to them every 365 days. It proves that there is still hope for them to change their ways."

"We'll see if you're right," said Alyak. "For now we'll leave Earth alone. We'll come back and revisit them to see if they have grown."

ALYAK AND RELYT FLEW AWAY
TO THEIR GALAXY FAR AWAY,
BUT WE NEVER KNOW WHEN
THEY MAY RETURN TO
CHECK ON US SOMEDAY.

Until then, try to remember
the message that they found.
The spirit of Christmas
can be with every one
of us year round.

CHRISTMAS REPRESENTS NEW
BEGINNINGS, HOPE, AND LOVE.
CARRY THESE WITH YOU
THROUGHOUT THE YEAR,
AND REMEMBER YOU'RE BEING
WATCHED BY SOMEONE ABOVE.

You've seen what the aliens in this story looked like. Use this page to draw your own original aliens!

Raccoons' Christmas

Written By Jay W. Foreman   Illustrated By Mark Sasser

If you enjoyed How Christmas Saved The World From Aliens, be sure to check out another Jay Foreman and Mark Sasser Holiday favorite, Raccoons' Christmas!

Printed by
EDWARDS BROTHERS
www.edwardsbrothers.com
11SKC10MDJa